What Our Readers Have Said...

Applicability

"These books are great tools that should be used as guidelines for our everyday supervisory practices. You need to take the time to do a short self-evaluation when reading them."

•

"The Pinpoint Training Series delivers information that could be used in a lot different areas."

•

"The things and problems we deal with everyday are discussed in these books."

Convenience

"I like this because I can take them with me to read at a convenient time. I feel the little time I have to spend in the office is best use on activities that directly relate to revenue opportunities. I like the short amount of time it takes to keep up with these."

•

"I prefer the self-study approach; it fits in with my schedule."

•

"I like the fact that the format allows the books to be reviewed as time permits. All work has been conducted on personal, evening/weekend time."

•

"Easy to use... if you put the time into it."

Challenge

"My thought is that the real value of these books comes into effect when doing the action plans."

•

"I like the fact that the format allows assignments to be reviewed as time permits."

Clarity

"Short and sweet. These books are easy to comprehend."

•

"Easy to use, understand, and reference if needed."

Relevance

"I have enjoyed reading these books. They are relevant to today's work environment and the ongoing change in the way we manage our workforce."

•

"I believe the contents of the Pinpoint series are excellent. It causes one to reflect on the daily dynamics in working with oneself as well as with management and peers."

Improving Workplace Interaction

Pinpoint Leadership Skill Development Training Series

TIMOTHY F. BEDNARZ

MAJORIUM
BUSINESS PRESS

Pinpoint Leadership Skill Development Training Series
"Improving Workplace Interaction"
Timothy F. Bednarz

Graphic design: Monika Pawlak

Majorium Business Press
2025 Main Street
Stevens Point, WI 54481
715.342.1018 • 800.654.4935

ISBN 978-1-882181-59-9

Printed in the United States of America

Introduction

The Pinpoint Leadership Skill Development Training Series is designed for targeted training and education regarding increased improvement in a specific skill or competency.

Each book within this series is designed to be easy to use, understand and apply to your job. It can be used as a basis for training individuals, as a discussion guide or as a personal training tool.

Each chapter within this book discusses a specific concept. When you have completed all eight chapters you should have a 360° perspective of the topic.

Additionally, each chapter is divided into specific sections:

- The first section provides you with an overview of the topic
- The Implications section discusses why the concept is important, and why it is important to learn and apply.
- The Strategies, Tips & Techniques to Apply section teaches how to use and apply the particular concept to your work.
- The Points to Ponder section gives you something to think about or to be discussed with a group setting. These are questions not meant to be immediately answered, but to be pondered over time.
- The Training Activity section provides you with the tools to transfer what you have learned to your job. It is designed to help create an action plan to effectively apply the concept.

Each of the topics in this series is time-tested and proven in the marketplace. They have been used by thousands of employees as training tools. Many of the users have commented that what made these books valuable, was the ability to refer to them when a problem surfaced. They indicated that they remembered reading about the exact problem. They referred back to these books and found an appropriate solution.

You will find them equally valuable as a resource in your professional development library.

Table of Contents

1. The Importance of Interacting Effectively with Employees 1

2. The Benefits of Interactive Leadership 7

3. Leadership by Example 11

4. Attention to Minor Details Prevents Major Problems 17

5. Employee Support Requires Interactive Leadership 21

6. Dealing with Negatively Interacting Employees 27

7. Interactive Decision Making.. 33

8. Helping Employees Succeed 39

LEARNING OBJECTIVES:

- To interpret and analyze the critical factors and benefits of interaction within an organization.
- To overcome problems and pitfalls related to leader and employee interaction.
- To apply specific strategies to enhance workplace interaction.
- To understand and identify the negative consequences of failing to develop effective interaction principles, practices and evaluation.
- To analyze the expected results and outcomes of developing and sustaining workplace interaction.
- To apply effective strategies to develop and enhance workplace, organizational and leadership interaction and interactivity.

1

The Importance of Interacting Effectively with Employees

Astute leaders guide and direct from the front lines of the company. Leaders are continually present and interacting with their employees in order to see what is slowly transforming and changing and what is causing unit frustrations. Frontline guiding and directing is a necessary process enabling leaders to apply their abilities to moving the organization forward.

There is a critical difference between the roles of a manager and a leader. While many managers are considered leaders, some not totally committed to sound leadership principles choose to direct from behind their desks. This results in relinquishing the advantage gained by immediate, firsthand knowledge of their organization's daily activities, progress or frustrating hindrances.

Ongoing interaction with employees is the active practice of visible leadership. Leaders cannot lead from their office. They must continually be in the midst of their employees, seeing for themselves what is happening and what is holding their unit back.

IMPLICATIONS — WHAT THIS MEANS TO YOU

Frontline guiding and directing is a critical concept for leaders to understand and apply. In order for employees to be comfortable with change and transformation within their organization and the constant risk taking that goes with it, leaders must be ever present to train, direct, and reassure each individual member. They must be there to cheer every accomplishment, no matter how small. This can only be done successfully when leaders are continually involved in their employees' daily activities.

STRATEGIES, TIPS & TECHNIQUES TO APPLY

Practical leadership demands that leaders have an active, ongoing presence within their organizational units. This presence creates a visible strength achieved through openly and consistently interacting with all employees. When leaders develop an interactive presence and work to achieve active visibility, they have the ability to fully apply their leadership skills and capabilities. Effective interaction allows leaders to:

Understand Frustrations

Only when leaders are constantly interacting with their employees can they fully understand the daily frustrations they are experiencing individually and as a group. While often minor, these frustrations serve as mini-barriers to productivity and efficiency.

Frustrations are often not known about unless a leader takes the time to observe what is actually occurring. They may be considered minor parts of the work process that employees fail to mention due to their insignificance. However, when considered collectively and cumulatively, smaller frustrations have the power to hemorrhage an organization's productivity.

Observe Firsthand What Is Occurring

Reports and meetings cannot take the place of the leader personally observing what is happening within their division or unit. A casual walkthrough does not provide sufficient opportunity to clearly observe and internalize what is actually occurring at any one point in time.

Close observation allows leaders to identify certain occurrences that produce either a positive or negative impact upon the organization. Only when leaders practice visible leadership and openly interact with their employees will a true picture of the organizational unit's overall progression and advancement emerge. Without this firsthand insight and knowledge, leaders cannot effectually move any part of their organization forward.

Encourage Open Communication

Visible leadership and open interactivity brings leaders out of their comfort zones and away from their desks. Being an interactive leader puts them on an equal plane with their employees, which makes them much more accessible and approachable. When this occurs, employees feel more comfortable to talk about frustrations, concerns, problems and issues that may not otherwise be disclosed. This open communication directly drives the free-flow of knowledge and information that leaders need to be successful.

Provide Insight into Solutions

When leaders become fully interactive, and observe and communicate with their employees, they gain insights into existing problems. Leaders use these insights to much more easily reach solutions to the immediate and pressing problems facing their employees. Minor frustrations are quickly remedied and eliminated to minimize productivity losses.

Change transformations in any organization entail countless daily decisions. Open interaction facilitates the decision making process by encouraging employees to make cooperative or independent judgments in the name of reaching objectives and eliminating needless frustrations.

Provide Insights into Problems and Opportunities

Leaders typically have the advantage of the "macro view" of their organization. Sometimes they are focused on this larger picture to the extent that they forget they can—and should—look for and watch what is actually transpiring in their front lines. While this field of vision will vary by the level occupied in the organization, leaders do have the advantage of obtaining increased knowledge through a wider perspective that is not available to their employees.

Leaders who are active and visible in their organizations have the ability to witness what is happening and can identify potential problems and opportunities because of it. Their position often allows them to act on this knowledge to either eliminate a potential problem or tap an opportunity. In either case a frontline perspective helps leaders and employees save their company money. The only sure way to accomplish any of the above is to take full advantage of applying all the available knowledge obtained from a more "micro view" of the organization.

Share in Successes and Failures

An essential role for leaders is to act as a motivator and cheerleader. While corporate leaders may not like to think of themselves as cheerleaders, the meaning goes beyond the term to the bottom line. When leaders are actively present and daily interacting with and encouraging their employees, they are in the best position to motivate and inspire them to achieve beyond expectations.

As their presence creates an impact on the organizational unit, leaders are able to share in the successes and failures of their employees as they test new ideas and concepts and help their organization adapt in the face of change. Doing this creates a bond of loyalty between leaders and employees as it steadily and securely increases the organizational unit's cohesiveness.

POINTS TO PONDER — SOMETHING TO THINK ABOUT

1. How present and visible are you within your organization on a day-to-day basis? Do you feel there is room for improvement?
2. Are you comfortable with the concept of continually interacting with all of your employees?

TRAINING ACTIVITY — APPLICATION & ACTION PLAN

List on a sheet of paper all of the things you were able to learn by being visible and openly interactive with your employees.

1. Identify the information you gained allowing you to identify potential problems and opportunities.
2. Identify minor problems and frustrations you were easily able to rectify.
3. Determine the value and impact of your interaction and visibility.

2

The Benefits of Interactive Leadership

Good leadership demands the use of every sense and communication ability to collect information, observe events, and develop a true "sense and feel" for what is happening in the organization. The alternative is to rely on secondhand observations and reports for the insights needed to make decisions and lead the organization. This flawed approach limits an individual leader's ability to effectively lead his or her organization.

The organizational environment is dynamic in the face of change and transformation. It is much akin to a battle because in many senses, every organization is in a fight for its survival. During a battle many events are occurring simultaneously, with the commander constantly receiving conflicting information and reports. Often the commander has an incomplete picture of the environment due to poor visibility clouded by events and terrain. Yet the military commander still must make life and death decisions based upon the information received and the observations they are able to make. This is the position many leaders in organizations find themselves in daily.

IMPLICATIONS — WHAT THIS MEANS TO YOU

Like a military commander, leaders must lead from the center of organizational activity in order to observe what is actually occurring and get an accurate sense of progress. In a dynamic environment, leaders must also be dynamic—and this will only occur when they practice interactive leadership. Only with this practice can leaders apply all of their physical senses to assist them to effectively make decisions and lead their employees.

STRATEGIES, TIPS & TECHNIQUES TO APPLY

The active, ongoing practice of interactive leadership is where the "rubber meets the road." This is where the principles of leadership are assembled and applied, and where a number of key benefits are derived including:

A 'Feel' for What Is Happening

Frontline employees in companies often have a stronger sense and feel for the business than many managers. They are regularly aware of the issues behind and solutions to many nagging frustrations. Many organizations refer to this as "native knowledge": a mine of information seldom tapped and shared simply because no one bothered to ask. (There are also employees who are reluctant to share their information, even when asked, fearing that it may be used against them.)

Effective leaders can only tap this valuable source of information by daily and visibly interacting with their frontline employees. Only then can they develop a true sense and feel for what is actually going on in their organization. This concept is known as "management by wandering around," and does have its detractors. However, effective leaders cannot develop a daily "nuts and bolts" understanding of their organization without it.

Reduced Information Distortion

Many managers like to have information fed to them in neat, cleanly packaged reports and PowerPoint presentations. The problem is that this information is frequently distorted by the natural bias of the author(s) and the filters applied to clean up the information. This is demonstrated by the old schoolyard game of "telephone" in which a number of individuals pass on a simple phrase to one another. Most often by the time the phrase reaches the last person it is completely distorted and has lost its original meaning—which is also true in the organizational environment. Information passed from individual to individual can often lose its original meaning and/or be "spun" to conform with a personal agenda or point of view. This presents a real danger to the decision maker in any organization because determinations are being made based upon faulty or biased information.

Leaders who actively practice interactive leadership deal with a significantly lower degree of information distortion because they are "in the trenches" and able to get direct information free of others' perspectives, filtering or personal agendas.

The importance of this leadership style cannot be overstated. Environments in organizations undergoing transformation in the face of change are not neat and tidy. Leaders contend with a frenetic pace introducing new variables at breakneck speed. This does not afford the luxury of waiting for filtered reports. It demands a leader's active presence to deal with these variables, events, problems and opportunities as they occur.

Increased Delegation and Empowerment

Often the concepts of delegation and empowerment are thought of in the broad sense of formal assignments, teams and committees. However, in the practical sense, as countless daily decisions are made in the face of change to transform the organization, the leader through the practice of visible leadership is able to delegate and empower employees, committees and work teams "on the fly" to handle minor decisions and correct nagging problems and frustrations. This effectively flattens layers of decision making and reduces functional barriers to taking action. Rather than wait for formal meetings to make these decisions, leaders can delegate and empower others to handle these variables and quickly move the organization forward.

When leaders become more effective in delegation and empowerment, it represents a major step in organizational development. These skills encourage the individual risk taking needed for change to occur as well as minimize many hindering barriers and frustrations. Delegation and empowerment increases employee motivation, responsiveness and productivity and transforms the unit environment from passive to proactive.

Better Informed Decision Making

Interactive leadership allows leaders to make better decisions because they have eliminated distorted information while improving their sense and feel for the organization. Through interactivity with their employees, leaders obtain multiple perspectives that provide additional insights to them. The more accurate the information and the more frontline feedback, the better qualified a leader is to make a decision.

POINTS TO PONDER — SOMETHING TO THINK ABOUT

1. Can you identify any additional benefits that the use and practice of interactive leadership offers?
2. Where do you consider yourself to be most effective when it comes to practicing the concept of interactive leadership?

TRAINING ACTIVITY — APPLICATION & ACTION PLAN

Take a prepared, secondhand report of a recent event or activity.

1. Compare the information in that report with your own personal knowledge of the event.
2. Cite the differences between what has been reported and what you have personally observed.
3. Determine the degree of information distortion in the report.
4. Identify ways this distortion can be minimized in the future.

3

Leadership by Example

A developmental milestone is reached when the leader is able to build trust and motivation with their employees to the degree that they are willing to openly follow their direction regardless of circumstances. This is not achieved until a leader is able to demonstrate—through personal example—that they have earned their employee's respect and admiration.

The practice of interactive leadership provides leaders with a distinct set of advantages that cannot be realized without their active presence. This enables them to establish trust, credibility and respect. These are all elements that buttress a leader's ability to personally lead their organization and motivate his or her employees to follow.

IMPLICATIONS – WHAT THIS MEANS TO YOU

It is one thing to lead an organization and quite another to motivate individuals to follow. The practice of interactive leadership demonstrates the character, ability and integrity of a leader and motivates individual employees to follow.

STRATEGIES, TIPS & TECHNIQUES TO APPLY

The practice of interactive leadership spotlights the individual leader and gives them the platform to shine by motivating their employees and effectively moving the organization forward. Interactive leadership is also the practice of leadership by example, and places all a leader says or does under the close scrutiny of their employees. Effective leaders use this to their advantage by practicing the following techniques:

Sell the Vision

In the storms of change and transformation, the leader's compass is his or her personal vision of the organization, its goals and potential accomplishments. Interactive leadership provides leaders with ample opportunities to "proselytize," or sell their vision to their employees every time the opportunity arises. This often means leaders are constantly talking about their vision and the positive changes that will take place when it is achieved.

The importance of a leader selling his or her vision cannot be overemphasized. As a leader, the goal is to motivate and lead employees. An essential part of motivation is selling employees on the vision and getting them to individually accept and "buy into" that vision as their own. Since organizational transformation in the face of change is normally a lengthy process, leaders must take every opportunity to remind their employees of the direction in which they are headed, and motivate them to continually work toward the accomplishment of their shared vision.

Walk the Talk

Interactive leadership places leaders under the microscope of employees who are continually assessing integrity and credibility. The practice of interactive management allows leaders to demonstrate their true character and build trust and loyalty with their employees. This is accomplished by a consistency in words and actions—the measure employees use to gauge a leader.

Consequently it is crucial for leaders to make certain they follow through on what they promise. If this is not possible, they have a good reason and take the time to explain why their promise cannot be kept.

Trust, credibility and loyalty are established when employees, associates and superiors know they can take what a leader says "to the bank," and that what he or she promises will be done. This trust is strengthened and a strong bond created when a leader clearly demonstrates by actions that he or she places their employee's interests above their own personal agenda.

Empower and Delegate

The practice of interactive leadership strengthens trust between leaders and employees when leaders actively empower employees and delegate tasks and assignments as needed. Empowering employees, groups and teams "on the fly" and delegating assignments when feasible allows leaders to swiftly respond to the rapid pace of change—as well as resolve problems and frustrations as or even before they occur.

Create Urgency

The rapid pace of change creates its own sense of urgency, but as transformation often takes time, leaders must motivate employees by further instilling this sense in them. This is best accomplished when leaders introduce new ideas and concepts, test them quickly, learn from the failures and move on to the next idea. It is through this process of continual adaptation and refinement of ideas and concepts that a sense of urgency is developed that keeps the organization moving forward toward transformation. In the absence of this sense of urgency it is easy for employees to fall into complacency.

Openly Communicating

Interactive leadership is built upon open communication and the ability of leaders to actively listen and respond to feedback and ideas offered by subordinates. This allows leaders to use all of their physical senses to observe and learn firsthand what is happening within their organization and to minimize the distortion of information.

Removing Obstacles

When leaders are ever-present and openly and actively interacting with their employees, they are able to identify and remove frustrations and barriers impeding forward movement.

Leaders openly empower their employees to overcome barriers and delegate the creation and implementation of the solution to them. Often these barriers come in the form of minor problems and issues that can be handled by frontline employees without the direct intervention of the leader. This enables the organization to be more responsive and productive.

Celebrate the Little Successes

The open presence of the leader among his or her employees allows them to plan for short-term wins and successes. These are important since the lengthy term of transformation can cause employees to lose sight of their goals and motivation. The celebration of short-term and minor successes maintains employee focus and keeps them motivated to continue to work toward the long-term success of the organization.

POINTS TO PONDER — SOMETHING TO THINK ABOUT

1. What do you do to lead by personal example?
2. What additional actions can you incorporate to demonstrate your interactive leadership commitment?

TRAINING ACTIVITY — APPLICATION & ACTION PLAN

1. Analyze the personal interactive leadership techniques you use to motivate employees to follow your lead and direction.
2. Review each of the following elements:
    - Selling the Vision
    - Walking the Talk
    - Empowering and Delegating

- Creating a Sense of Urgency
- Communicating Openly
- Removing Obstacles
- Celebrating All Successes

3. List on a sheet of paper each of the elements cited above.
4. Identify what you personally do to actively practice each of these within your department and organization.
5. Identify what additional activities and/or actions you can incorporate to increase practice of the above elements.

4

Attention to Minor Details Prevents Major Problems

The saying, "the devil is in the details" is true in all organizational and business environments. Often when leaders take the time to empower their employees and teams to handle minor details and problems, major problems are avoided or at least minimized.

As has been emphasized in previous lessons, the process of transformation and change with an organization demands that countless decisions be made on a daily basis. The concept of effective leadership drives decisions lower within the organization to the front lines so that decisions can be made quickly where and when they count. While leaders must be in the midst of their organization monitoring what is happening and assisting where needed, they cannot be omnipresent, nor can they make all decisions required to make the organization run smoothly.

IMPLICATIONS — WHAT THIS MEANS TO YOU

It is vital that leaders enable and rely on employees to handle details and small problems on their own, as these are the situations and circumstances where trust and empowerment are formed. An atmosphere of trust encourages and empowers employees to take risks and make decisions "on the fly" when they are needed. Often many of these minor decisions directly impact both their workplace and productivity by resolving nagging problems and frustrations—and avoiding major problems later on.

STRATEGIES, TIPS & TECHNIQUES TO APPLY

Leaders must understand that as they cannot be omnipresent they have the tools of delegation, empowerment and trust at their disposal to extend their reach to all corners of the organization. While they can and should be present within the organization and actively interacting with their employees, they must also trust their people to solve problems and frustrations without their direct intervention, unless the issue is beyond the scope of the employee's/workgroup's responsibility.

Empowering individuals to resolve issues before they blossom into larger and more expensive problems to solve also frees the leader to address more important problems and responsibilities.

Delegate and Empower

Leaders must create a positive atmosphere of trust where minor problems, details and issues can be effectively resolved by individual frontline employees, workgroups and teams. While this process may start slowly, especially when it hasn't been freely employed in the past, leaders and employees must develop a growing bond of trust allowing them to make more tactical decisions, with the leader daily interacting and monitoring activities.

Push Decision Making to the Frontline Employee

Regardless of their capacity or station, the frontline employee must be trained to be the eyes of the organization. These employees have an up close gritty and extremely useful perspective of what is happening "in the trenches" of the organization. Once trained, they see what is happening and what is causing problems and frustrations, where in the past they might have either ignored these concerns out of fear or apathy or reported them and hoped for the best. Now rather than waiting for the bureaucratic process to resolve problems, or being reluctant, leaders have equipped their people to generate solutions "on the fly."

Encourage and Reward Risk Taking

When decision making is driven downward to frontline employees, levels of reluctance and fear may surface. There will be fear of the repercussions of making the wrong decision, especially if a more risk-adverse environment existed in the past. Each individual decision has some risk associated with it. There is always the likelihood that the decision will be wrong, further complicating the problem.

Leaders must foster an atmosphere where employees are encouraged to make careful decisions regardless of circumstances. In every situation employees consider all aspects of their decisions and associated risks. They make informed decisions based upon their personal experience, expertise and the available information shared with them.

Learn from Mistakes and Failures

While employees are being cultivated to make informed decisions, it is easy to review the basis for decisions and the reasons why they may have turned out poorly. Once looked at, lessons can be derived from the mistake or failure. Within the confines of a learning organization, mistakes and failures should be encouraged since this is only how employees can learn and grow.

Organizations with zero-tolerance for mistakes and failures are only fooling themselves, as even of course with these rigid standards, mistakes and failures happen—and are often hidden from managers and leaders. These poor outcomes fester into bigger problems, often blindsiding leadership later and derailing any or much of the progress made.

POINTS TO PONDER — SOMETHING TO THINK ABOUT

1. What is your tolerance level for mistakes and failures made by your employees?
2. How much do you trust your employees to make effective decisions and resolve problems on their own?

TRAINING ACTIVITY — APPLICATION & ACTION PLAN

Examine your organization to determine ways it can foster higher levels of delegation and empowerment in order for employees to handle minor decisions, problems and frustrations as they arise.

1. Determine the various levels where current decisions are made.
2. Identify ways to drive decision making down to your front line employees.
3. Determine ways to reward individual decision making and risk taking.

5

Employee Support Requires Interactive Leadership

Effective leadership is an active, not passive, process. Leaders get involved in the day-to-day challenges and inspire employees to take risks and rise above the ordinary in their thinking, attitudes and actions. Leaders know they are not always the innovators, and believe that workplace innovations and especially daily task-related decisions should be made by the employees doing the work. They fully support the actions of their employees and see that they are given the opportunity to create, innovate, and adopt new ideas and methods.

One of a leaders primary tasks is to develop a sincere interactive leadership style and work climate focused on their employees' advancement and attainment of goals. Creating a supportive work atmosphere becomes a main ingredient for achievement. Without daily interactive leadership support, very little gets accomplished within an organization.

IMPLICATIONS – WHAT THIS MEANS TO YOU

A totally supportive leadership climate implies establishing shared power, shared risk and shared accountability. It visibly supports all employees' actions through mutual respect and trust. Only in this way will there be a willingness on the employees' part to make the organization a top priority with a shared desire to strengthen it.

Interactive leadership focuses on making the organization's welfare the number one priority by cultivating each and every employee to support its direction and efforts. Supportive leaders continually emphasize the fact that if the organization wins, everyone wins. Every employee activity that assists and promotes this belief must be nurtured and encouraged.

STRATEGIES, TIPS & TECHNIQUES TO APPLY

The thrust of leadership is to support all employees effectively and passionately enough to instill the belief and trust that attainment of collective goals will benefit all involved. To see employees reach this level of trust and security, leaders can do the following:

Link Collective and Management Goals

It is essential that interactive leaders support their employees in all their efforts, especially when it comes to identifying and attaining goals. Before goals can become a reality, leaders must instill in their employees a desire and passion to think in terms of the organization's best interest. Organizations and companies do not just "pocket profits," they provide people and families with jobs with which to earn a living. It is in this light that every activity and action needs to be focused on the organization's advancement.

In order to best support their employees in this effort, leaders must make certain that they develop specific strategies for linking management goals to all individual and collective employee goals. In this way, as the organization succeeds, so do they.

Build a Mutual Interactive Support Network

Interactive leadership and its support is a relationship between leaders and the employees they seek to lead. A failure to understand that leadership is a shared responsibility easily breaks down the support process being actively built within an organization.

Interactive leaders don't attempt to become heroes by accepting full responsibility for their departments, thinking they should be aware of everything going on and able to solve every problem that arises. They realize this mindset inhibits personal and employee progress and development. It disintegrates the shared vision intended to direct, guide and support every unit member toward each goal's attainment.

Help Employees Realize Their Goals are Cooperative

Leaders interactively support their employees by helping them realize that their goals are cooperative. This is accomplished through applying day-to-day organizational norms, expectations and standards that encourage them to share information, consider each other's ideas, exchange resources, and respond to each other's requests through positive interdependence. Doing this ensures the building of a mutually interactive employee support network.

Effective leaders plant "seed" questions that require employees to gather input from peers before responding. This technique serves to create an environment of active communication on all levels, which instills a high degree of mutual support within the specific organizational unit.

Offer Direct Help and Provide Necessary Resources

Providing ongoing, direct assistance and the resources needed to do the job are concrete signs of cooperative goal attainment. Imparting information on how a newer technology might facilitate completion of an assignment, or offering suggestions as to how to increase personal productivity or decrease wasted time and energy are visible examples of a leader's desire to actively support all members of their work unit.

This strategy also serves to unify the entire unit, as it actively promotes the general welfare of the employee as well as the organization. It emphasizes that even though assignments vary, everyone has the same basic goal. All tasks and individuals become interdependent in the name of advancing the leader's vision and organization's cause.

Distorting or withholding information is a clear sign that an active undermining of a leader is taking place within the organization. This destabilizes the motivational framework within individual work units. It also instills a sense of competition between leader and employees, and manifests a lack of trust on the leader's part.

Promote Cooperation

Leaders support each individual member in words and actions demonstrating respect, warmth and personal acceptance. They resist the urge to make competitive comparisons among employees. Effective interactive leaders reward productive individual and cooperative efforts to develop and attain specific goals and objectives.

The key to moving the organization forward lies not in promoting competition, showing preference for one employee over another or overpowering people to gain compliance, but in winning their employees' complete cooperation, trust and loyalty.

In order to do this, leaders must foster an atmosphere that secures collective participation among their employees. Actively supporting cooperation built on mutual interdependence is the most effective strategy for creating and sustaining strong collaborative relationships. This strategy is successful because it demonstrates both a willingness to be cooperative and an unwillingness to be taken advantage of.

Interactive leaders need to recognize and encourage ongoing positive interaction among employees. This implies actively working to instill cooperative reciprocity that establishes deeper bonds of trust. During this process employees begin to openly acknowledge that all goals and work-related assignments are collaboratively essential and equally important.

One of the most effective strategies for eliciting cooperative efforts and to display active employee support is to enlarge the "screen of the future." In other words, leaders must promote the realization among employees that they can expect to be working together as an ongoing group in all future assignments, tasks, decision making, goal setting and planning.

Employees are much more likely to support one another and their leader when they know they will be involved with each other on a continual basis. This is because an expectation of future interaction encourages employees to actively support and cooperate with one another in the present. Active support on all levels becomes far more common and enduring.

POINTS TO PONDER — SOMETHING TO THINK ABOUT

1. Does your leadership style produce a mutually supportive process of employee interaction?
2. Have you developed cooperation among your employees based upon a mutual desire for sustaining collaborative relationships?

TRAINING ACTIVITY — APPLICATION & ACTION PLAN

1. Refer to the supportive strategies below. Use them to increase higher levels of employee cooperation, interdependency, trust and security.
    - Link collective and management goals.
    - Build a mutually interactive support network.
    - Help employees realize their goals are shared.
    - Offer direct help and provide the needed resources.
    - Promote cooperation.
2. List some strategies you can apply to increase employee support within your departmental work unit in each of these areas. Brainstorm with your employees for input as to what other activities and strategies may work to develop a more comprehensive, cooperative support system.

6

Dealing with Negatively Interacting Employees

Effectively addressing negative employee interaction requires singling out what truly engages the minds, actions and hearts of individuals. Leaders must identify the factors producing the need in some employees to act negatively and callously toward others. In almost all cases, negative interaction among employees is the result of functioning in a less than meaningful workplace. To stifle interactive negativity, leaders must identify both the factors defining and methods creating a meaningful, reciprocal work environment.

It is important for leaders to understand every employee has a personal set of factors defining a meaningful workplace. When leaders fail to apply practical strategies for making the workplace more reciprocal, with people respectfully and productively working toward a common goal, they can expect continuous negative interaction among employees. This creates havoc that slows productivity and advancement for both the individual work unit and the organization.

How employees define a meaningful work environment determines how they function within their current environment. Some factors are more important than others. For one employee, the top factors may be a desire for a deep sense of purpose, the freedom to be innovative, and the opportunity to build strong relationships in the work setting. Another's factors might include ownership in ideas and solutions, an atmosphere that encourages overcoming challenges or a feeling of success within the work unit.

IMPLICATIONS — WHAT THIS MEANS TO YOU

The leadership challenge for reducing and eliminating employee interactive negativity is to reflect on what it is that makes a work environment truly rewarding and fulfilling. Leaders need to create a workplace that keeps its employees busy and productive, but one that also keeps their minds and hearts actively engaged. The only way personal negativity and accompanying actions are displaced is with security, trust, comradery, positive interaction and mutual respect.

STRATEGIES, TIPS & TECHNIQUES TO APPLY

Leaders assess their workplace and put into word and action what employees desire to see in a meaningful and rewarding environment. In order to do this, leaders:

Conduct an Environmental Climate Check

Leaders analyze their own negative feelings regarding the workplace. They ask, "Do I often find myself dwelling on the negative aspects of my work and performance and the atmosphere that exists?" If the answer is "yes," the reasons behind their feelings are a good indicator of why employees feel the same way and negative interactions are taking place.

Taking the time to complete an analysis of the entire work unit atmosphere is the first step in dealing with negative employee interaction. In order to effect positive workplace change, leaders should both ask themselves the following questions and take appropriate actions wherever a "yes" response exists:

- Is there an unspoken understanding that work should always be first in every employee's life?
- Does the organizational culture favor workaholics?
- Do employees that don't share this "work first" philosophy feel guilty?
- Is there undue pressure on employees to make trade-offs with tasks

and assignments against time, resources and availability?

- Do individual assignments have more importance than collaborative efforts, trial-and-error methods and interactive positive communication?
- Is praise a lower priority than the completion of timelines and tasks?

Seek Out Specific Areas in Which to Focus Your Efforts

Every organizational work unit has room for improvement. The key rests in a leader's ability to know where to focus his or her efforts for maximum effect. The following are actions proven to transform the work environment in the quickest and most effective way:

- Finding out what is most important to employees as far as creating a non-threatening, secure and fulfilling work environment.
- Understanding each employee's top priorities as they relate to work and themselves personally. This can be the starting point for creating a more meaningful and productive workplace for all.
- Allowing employees to pause after a major completed task or project in order to gain a sense of closure and to savor their accomplishments.
- Acknowledging all progress and getting upper management to recognize major milestones and hurdles employees reach and overcome.
- Making challenges exciting, somewhat demanding, but realistic.
- Allowing employees to make best use of their talents and to freely use others whenever needed as resources for input, ideas and suggestions.

Track the Fit of Your Employees

Getting to know what fires up your employees is crucial in fostering a rewarding work environment. Identifying the skills and talents they have outside the workplace can help place them into a better fit inside the organization. One of a leader's responsibilities is to find out what their employees' interests are, or their sources of motivation and energy. It is vital to talk to each employee about their passions, talents and creative abilities, and then tap into them however and whenever possible.

Negativity permeates an employee's attitudes when they feel misplaced in their jobs, tasks, assignments and responsibilities. In order to overcome this, leaders assess:

- Whether the big picture of the organization is thoroughly discussed with employees so that they clearly understand their personal place in it and how they specifically factor into its success.
- If there are any employees who feel a particular job or assignment "just isn't right" for them. It is important to find out what employees feel they can take on more capably, then match them with projects, assignments, and duties where they can better achieve success.
- If there are some employees who feel a clash between their values and goals and those of others in the workplace. When work makes employees feel they need to be a different person in order to "fit in," a leader can expect negative employee interactions to occur repeatedly.
- Whether employees are allowed to consistently tap into their strengths and spend a great deal of their assignment time in activities best matched to their interests and talents.

Analyze Your Unit's Flexibility

Nothing creates more negative interaction among employees than a work environment that remains inflexible to their needs. Leaders need to establish a more meaningful work environment by making certain that flexibility exists for all employees. They need to make sure the corporate rulebook does not overshadow the positive accomplishments taking place within the unit and among its members. Leaders need to consider:

- Are work unit rules flexible when certain situations arise, or are they rigid to the point where the rulebook is still the ultimate word?
- Are policies and procedures followed to the letter without allowing employees to question their validity and necessity?
- In order to accomplish certain things do employees feel they must sidestep rules and hope they don't get caught?

Addressing and changing areas needing improvement allows leaders to spend more of their time doing that which works to motivate employees and move the organization forward. Strengthening these areas is best accomplished by interacting with every employee, and taking action to build stronger personal relationships and subsequently a more secure, meaningful workplace.

POINTS TO PONDER — SOMETHING TO THINK ABOUT

1. Do you feel much of the negative interaction among employees is due to feeling uncomfortable, insecure and unsuccessful in their jobs and performance?
2. Knowing the work climate that exists in your unit, do you feel you know where to focus your efforts first, in order to create a more meaningful work environment and counteract the negativity within it?

TRAINING ACTIVITY — APPLICATION & ACTION PLAN

Begin to design a more meaningful workplace for your employees. Do this by:

1. Conducting an environmental "climate check."
2. Seeking out specific areas to focus your efforts upon.
3. Tracking the "fit" of your employees.
4. Analyzing your unit's flexibility.

7

Interactive Decision Making

Success in the workplace depends on individuals working together to make decisions promoting the common purpose and welfare of the unit and organization. This is not easily accomplished, because the process is subject to the ups and downs of human interaction, and thus there will always be unexpected eruptions of conflict, disagreement and resistance. Interactive decision making is well worth the frustration and energy. When decisions are reached through mutual efforts, they are fully accepted and adhered to.

In considering interactive decision making, one area leaders often fall short in is asking for and receiving input from employees regarding possible solutions, then deciding themselves what is best for the unit or organization.

While there is some employee participation when this occurs, the decisions made by the leader will never be fully approved by all members of the unit or deemed worthy of total acceptance. When leaders resort to this practice they actually negate the concept of interactive decision making altogether. They do more harm when this happens because they feign using employee input and destroy their trust. In the employees' eyes the leader belittles their intelligence and capabilities.

IMPLICATIONS — WHAT THIS MEANS TO YOU

In order to master the art of incorporating interactive decision making into daily operations, leaders must rely on a proactive leadership style that supports cooperation and full participation rather than telling and selling employees on decisions they themselves choose to make.

STRATEGIES, TIPS & TECHNIQUES TO APPLY

When leaders make decisions by themselves they must resort to defending the "why's" of their actions. When interactive decision making takes place, the problem of having to sell employees on why a decision was made or how something should be done isn't a factor—it has already been defined by consensus.

The interactive decision making process focuses on allowing each participant the voice and freedom to raise questions in order to analyze and expand upon shared information. Once the group has acquired enough collective knowledge, the members act upon it and generate a specific solution. Leaders facilitate the process in the following ways:

Managing the Decision Making Process

Interactive decision making needs to be managed as carefully as any other company system because it has the potential to create as well as solve problems. To manage the first phase of the interactive decision making process the leader should:

- Share thoughts on the problem at hand. Include the factors bringing the situation about. Speak to why it needs addressing from a decision making standpoint. Getting employees' input and reactions is the main focus here.
- Suggest a tentative solution to the problem. Request additional insight into the problem and ask employees to react and comment on it.
- Ask, "Does anyone have a better solution?" and let the ideas flow.

Addressing the How to of Making Effective Interactive Decisions

The most significant part of interactive decision making is that leaders and upper management genuinely desire the input of their employees. They are not merely going through the motions of asking for it without the intention to use and apply it. They trust that their employees have the knowledge and skill to make good decisions. Because of this belief leaders support their cooperation and help implement the results of their efforts.

There are specific steps leaders can take to strengthen employee involvement in the decision making process as well as the solutions generated:

- Seek input and direction from employees directly impacted by the decision.
- Seriously and objectively consider possible outcomes and ramifications of a particular problem together as a total work unit.
- Utilize only the ideas everyone agrees represent the best of the total number generated.
- Give credit and other appropriate rewards to those whose ideas were used.
- Make certain those whose ideas were rejected know their ideas were carefully considered. At this stage it is important to explain the reasons why one idea "won out" over another. The leader can then tell the group something akin to the fact that "(thought or concept) was a good idea. Let's take another look at it when a similar situation surfaces."

Creating a Problem Solving Meeting

One other option leaders have for decision making is to hold an interactive problem solving meeting. This is more of an informal approach to making decisions. Interactivity is dependent on smaller groups ranging from three to five participants. Problem solving meetings are often good when:

- Decisions need to be made "on the fly" as they surface.
- Participants have some training in the decision making process itself.
- The leader facilitates the meeting and strives to get members to reach a consensus on a single, effective solution.
- The leader selects participants who will be directly affected by the problem needing resolution.

The most important prerequisite for any genuinely interactive decision making process is that it is never something middle management is ordered to carry out. With this philosophy any interactive decision making attempts will fail.

The process must start with the top believing interactive participation is important. Top management and its leadership must actively support the process by taking action to implement the solutions employees generate to move the work unit and organization forward.

POINTS TO PONDER — SOMETHING TO THINK ABOUT

1. Have you ever asked for input from employees about possible problems and solutions, but once receiving it, turned around and decided what was best on your own? If so, what problems did it create?
2. Do you prefer a more formal approach to interactive decision making, or an informal one? Why?

TRAINING ACTIVITY — APPLICATION & ACTION PLAN

Analyze to see how you personally manage the beginning portion of an interactive decision making session. Ask yourself the questions below.

- Do you share your thoughts on the problem, including detailing the factors that brought the situation about?
- Do you cover with your employees why a problem needs addressing from a decision making standpoint?
- Do you solicit adequate employee input and reaction?
- Do you suggest a tentative solution to the problem?

- Do you request additional insight into the problem and ask employees to react and comment on it?
- Do you ask whether anyone has a better solution or an idea to help formulate a specific course of action?
- Do you let the ideas begin to flow and allow employees to define, analyze, create and agree on an effective solution?

8

Helping Employees Succeed

Aiding employees in achieving their personal goals and feeling important and successful within the organization requires good interactive leadership practices. Effective leaders consider helping their employees to be successful an exciting, worthwhile pursuit. When employees are successful, so are leaders.

Helping employees succeed is essential to keeping work units, projects and the entire organization running smoothly and on course. It is not unlike an environment where employees are novice pioneers, dependent upon leaders to guide the wagon train through the chaotic and ever-changing organizational wilderness into "the promised land."

Achieving and attaining the "unordinary" is the major force behind moving individuals ahead, as it instills a sense of organizational worth and the attainment of incremental successes. In moving employees forward leaders must continually build and instill a desire and commitment to persevere, while continually looking toward the horizon rather than backward.

IMPLICATIONS – WHAT THIS MEANS TO YOU

If leaders fail in their responsibility to harness the best they and their employees can give, all actions get caught up in trivial, daily routines and procedures, problems and issues. Concentrating on the "ordinary" militates against successful achievement and accomplishment.

Individual and cooperative encouragement is the means to goal attainment that is "beyond the ordinary." An interactive leader's experience, insight and carefully applied strategies avoid many of the overwhelming barriers and frustrations that wait in hiding. These are vital to eliminate because they can automatically dampen an employee's spirit and the desire to continue onward toward the achievement of success.

STRATEGIES, TIPS & TECHNIQUES TO APPLY

In order to help their employees succeed, leaders employ specific strategies to reinforce motivation, determination and perseverance. These include:

Use New Assignments to Test Individual and Cooperative Limits

It is a leader's responsibility to remain alert for ways to improve their work unit's productivity and the organization itself. This depends on giving full support to their employees; they are the ones possessing the skills and manpower required to make improvements a reality.

There is no better way to achieve success than by openly testing individual and workgroup limits. Isolating a difficult job situation and placing employees or groups directly into it provides leaders a revealing gauge of their capabilities. It is also an effective way to overcome a negative problem or situation plaguing the unit or organization. Once accomplished, it instills a feeling of success, self-worth, and the desire to tackle other challenging projects and assignments. The group/individuals begin to realize they can "accomplish the nearly impossible" by merely challenging, pushing and extending their limits. Consistent encouragement is given during the entire interactive process to see the challenge through.

A leader's active support during this process is used to encourage his or her people and instill a sense of adventure into the assignment. This is key to making any challenge more enjoyable and successful. Without developing a pioneer spirit of determination and fortitude to surmount the challenges new assignments present, existing fears and uncertainty become an overwhelming obstacle. "Going where no one has gone before" and getting there with whatever it takes is a stimulating way for leaders and their employees to approach each new assignment.

Consistently Question the Status Quo

Facilitating their employees' success requires that a leader continually urge them to challenge certain processes and offer suggestions on how unproductive efforts or inefficiencies can be improved upon. In order to accomplish this, they list all current work practices within their unit or organization. These must be firmly established and in the category of "the way it's always been done." Once the list is compiled they turn it over to their employees and ask, "How useful is each practice for doing the best we can?"

This interactive technique generates creativity and innovation among employees because they are empowered to determine whether or not a particular process or way of performing tasks or assignments is efficient or essential. The critical part of the procedure is to carefully analyze and evaluate the impact of each process and form or structure of task assignment to determine whether any should be kept in place, altered or eliminated.

If certain procedures are selected for modification or possible elimination, the challenge is to find a way to change it. (Policies critical to productivity and quality assurance cannot be challenged and are out of bounds for analyzing and assessing.) Success comes when employees are able to eliminate generally useless rules and needless routines that only hinder their abilities, performance and jobs.

Break Free of the Routine

Nothing stymies success more than becoming robots of routine. Comfort zones are the greatest inhibitors of thinking, creativity and innovation, which are indispensable to success.

To help free employees of their comfort zones leaders can use the following exercise. Have employees make a complete list of their daily habits, activities and routines. Ask them to respond to the question, "Which of these improve my feeling of self-worth and my efforts in the unit and organization, and which do not?"

Have them circle the "helping" activities and place a check mark next to those that are "hindering." If they have a difficult time determining whether they actually want to eliminate some of the hindrances they should be told to ask themselves, "If I keep on with this particular habit, activity or routine, what is the worst that can happen?" After responding, employees should ask the question positively, "What is the best thing that can happen to me if I eliminate this particular hindrance?"

Finally, employees ask, "How successful will I feel knowing that I can overcome something that hinders me? How will it improve my outlook to know I have control over things that prevent me from moving ahead?"

In supporting employees in their efforts to overcome hindering practices and habits, success can be brought about in incremental steps with minimal amounts of effort. The goal is to displace useless habits deeply entrenched in comfort zones with more productive ones. Leaders and employees will both find that the growth pains are clearly worth the gain in creativity, innovation, overall personal productivity and job satisfaction.

POINTS TO PONDER — SOMETHING TO THINK ABOUT

1. Are you making employee assignments a "pioneering" experience?
2. What other techniques can you use to actively support moving employees out of their established comfort zones?

TRAINING ACTIVITY — APPLICATION & ACTION PLAN

1. Find out what motivates each of your employees to be more productive in their job and what instills a feeling of success in them.
2. Begin by incorporating strategies that work to encourage and support your employees' efforts to attain success. Add other techniques after success in these areas has been attained.
    - Treating new assignments as a means to test individual and cooperative limits
    - Actively and consistently questioning the status quo
    - Breaking free of the routine

About the Author

Timothy F. Bednarz, Ph.D. is CEO of the American Management Development Group, Inc. For over 20 years he has researched, designed and authored hundreds of learning and development programs used by Fortune 1000 companies.

He is also the author of *Great! What Makes Leaders Great. What They Did, How They Did It and What You Can Learn from It* (2011).

Speaking Availability

Timothy F. Bednarz, Ph.D. is available for speaking engagements for your next meeting or association event. He can be contacted at 800-654-4935 or by e-mail at timothy.bednarz@majorium.com.

Bulk Sales

Bulk sales of this book or any other titles available from Majorium Business Press. Inquiries can be directed to sales@majorium.com, or by phone at 800-6654-4935.

Quick Order Form

Fax orders: 715-342-1118. Send this form.

Telephone orders: Call 800-654-4935 toll-free. Have your credit card ready.

Email orders: sales@majorium.com

Postal orders: Majorium Business Press, 2025 Main Street, Stevens Point, WI 54481, USA.

Please send the following books:

____

____

____

____

Please send more FREE information on:

❑Catalog ❑Speaking/Seminars ❑Mailing Lists ❑Consulting

Name: ____________________________________

Address: __________________________________

City: ____________________ State: _____ Zip: ________

Telephone: ________________________________

Email address: _____________________________

Sales tax: Please add 5.5% for products shipped to Wisconsin addresses.

Shipping by air:

United States: $4.00 for first book and $2.00 for each additional product.

International: $9.00 for first book; $5.00 for each additional product (estimate).

Made in United States
Cleveland, OH
06 November 2026

47678349R10030